Across My Silence

by

Jack Cooper

ISBN 978-1-934209-37-0

10-digit ISBN 1-934209-37-6

$15.99

© 2007, World Audience, Inc.

Cover design and art by Christopher Taylor (ctaylor5uk@yahoo.co.uk). For this particular cover, the artist used photography (leaves), illustration – a mixture of water colour paints and Tria graphics pens (butterfly) and digital methods to add water and lighting.

World Audience (www.worldaudience.org) is a global consortium of artists and writers, producing the literary journal *audience* and *The audience Review*. Our periodicals and books are edited by M. Stefan Strozier and assistant editors. Please submit your stories, poems, paintings, photography or other artwork to submissions@worldaudience.org. Inquire about being a reviewer: theatre@worldaudience.org. Thank you.

Across My Silence

by

Jack Cooper

A World Audience Book

(www.worldaudience.org)

February 2007

New York

be unto love as rain is unto colour;
E. E. Cummings

Across My Silence is for my mother and father.

TABLE OF CONTENTS

Introduction..9
Across My Silence...11
Before Dawn...12
Among the Creatures..13
This Welling Up...15
The Church of April Morning..16
Broken..17
Monday Morning...18
16 Cents..19
As Long As It Takes..20
Tandem Life..21
Long Shadows...22
Jesus at the Chevron...23
Fragment of the Day 24
Somewhere in the Valley..25
Menagerie..26
A Morning of Nothing...27
Half Myself...28
Roused..29
Guys With Guns...31
Dry Lightning..31
Existential Market..33
South of Sunset...35
Uneasy Pairings...36
Passerby..37
Leaving for Somewhere..38
No Longer..39
For Us Both..40
Witness...41
At Some Point...42
Scant Light...43
At the Lake...44
Gnarled...45
Rosebud..46
Sayonara, My Love..47
Pearl Nebula...48
A Little Jazz..49
Season After...50

Hitting the Wall...52
Into Our Time..53
Runoff...54
The Proposal...55
Only Once..56
Flight Path...57
Garden to Garden..58
Just After...59
Unforgotten...60
First Light..61
Transition..62
Re-creation..63
Fire..64
Danger of Fire..65
Fire in Me..66
A Good Stick..67
Feast of Impulse..68
The Turtles of La Escobilla...69
The Thought of Being..70
Party..71
Tidepool...72
Footprints..73
Egret..74
Pangolin...75
Restless..76
Lollypop...77
There is a Listening..78
Dissembled..79
Elm in Dirt With Bird...80
Wouldn't it be Nice..81
Cricket...82
Lizard...83
From Time to Time...84
Break...85
Lingering Star..86
Open Window...87
A Moon or Two...88
The Long Forgetting...89
One Orange Eye...90
Self-circumference...92
Transitory Endings...93
Some People..95

Even One...96
Good News/ Bad News...97
Calling Back...98
Touch and Go..99
Limb..100
Sky..101
Edge of Time..102
Obituary..104
Disappearances...105
Over a Shoulder..106
A Guy I Grew Up With...108
The Fall...109
In This Life..110
Shoulders...111
To Mention Rain...112
No One Else..113
Letter From Elsewhere...114
Absolutely..116
In His Honor...117
Elegy Among Shadows..118
The Reader...119
The Mountain...120
Far Field..121
Reading Lorca..122
This Morning I Wake Up...123
Birdhouse..124
Home..125
Friends..126
Voyager...127
Art in the Universe..129
Anything but Now..130
In the Absence of Thumbs...132
Jack Cooper's Biography...135
Acknowledgements..136

INTRODUCTION

Revived by a Sparkling Poet

Vladimir Nabokov never read the poems of Jack Cooper but one guesses at his delight. It is in Cooper's collection, *This Welling Up,* that we find the very inspired writing that Nabokov described when he said, "You experience a shuddering sensation of wild magic, of some inner resurrection, as if a dead man were revived by a sparkling drug that has been rapidly mixed in your presence."

I find that I am that dead man before I enter the world of Cooper's magic. I turn from my beige, flatland life of petty concerns into his pages unsuspecting. And his lure is crafty. Cooper puts his arm around the reader's shoulder and walks him in to a world not unlike my own, average and desperate, until the first flash happens. That's when his writing revives us all.

As in his poem "Transitory Endings" where poet and reader link up and identify at the grim nexus of "this life of fitful births and small deaths" only to feel a surge of inspired shared warmth, as we see that we are "people warming up to the future together/like family, like birds" and even more deeply connected in the end knowing "that whatever happens/ is created by everyone" and "We are all finishing/ each other's stories."

Cooper's poetic landscape is usually urban California, with an occasional sense of the City of Angels. Yet the beauty that startles you, like a friend's gentle punch to the heart, comes from far away, and sweeps us into the "one mind" we all share, appearing in "Disappearances" as "the wide river of light/ that keeps the world from ending."

One need not be a passionate conservationist or lover of animals to be charmed by Cooper's admiration of them. The awe he feels in "The Turtles of La Escobilla" for the turtles' unstoppable life force in the face of human cruelty runs deeper than an environmentalist's tantrum. And that, in the end, is the deep place where only poetry can go. Beyond the topical and beyond the political into the eternal. Cooper's poems are all tickets to that deep place.

In "Gnarled" Cooper's sparse craft and cutting humor give tribute to Charles Bukowski, the prolific prose vulgarian whose prodigious talent Cooper mirrors. Like Bukowski, Cooper traffics in everyday squalor and grit. But unlike Bukowski, Cooper transcends. He moves along the ground with Bukowski's eye for the beauty in the swirling streets but more than once in each poem Cooper soars back up where Bukowski never went, to a sublime height where he sees and illuminates "time, unbuckled from its human wrist,/ set free to explore alternatives".

Jack Cooper is a surprising poet. Unafraid to lure us with guileless, plainspoken verse, he is also as unafraid to take us into a verse inhabited by Rimbaud, Kant and Sir Isaac Newton. These moments are often like the floor dropping out of an elevator. They are unexpected when you're inside the poem, but soon they are exactly and always what you expect whenever you open the book of his work.

I was a Creative Writing Major at the University of Arizona studying under the wonderful poets Richard Shelton and Steve Orlen. Later I went on to become a writer of advertising copy, song lyrics, books on business and the psychology of success, and after all the years of perverting and prostituting one's poetic yearning, what a blessed gift it has been to read the poems of Jack Cooper. It's a return to that wide river of light that keeps the world from ending.

Stephen D. Chandler
Author, *The Story of You*

ACROSS MY SILENCE

Beyond probability
your arms move
across my silence
like summer moves
meadow by meadow
up the mountain,
no corolla uncovered,
no shadow alone.

Opening everywhere
the hearts
of small lost voices,
you reinvent me
in your gentleness
quantum by quantum
thought by thought,
like summer is a thought
buried in the snow
imagining your waist.

You are why it's
so hard to believe
that sunlight can be frozen,
that most of everything
is darkness,
that whatever
cannot be measured
cannot be there.

BEFORE DAWN

I like the world before dawn
when nothing has been decided yet,
not the meaning of yesterday,

not the fate of tomorrow.
Some of the birds have a clue it's true
but most of creation isn't sure

how to read the leaves.
Even the cat doesn't know
where it's going to nap all day.

I like to throw open my window
to a big moon medallion
on the long dark neck

of the sky above the garden.
I like the way silence prevails
in the workplace of spiders and bats

and a vast stillness gathers around
as if I were witness to some secret
ceremony of the elements,

hooded spirits preparing to bless
the birth of the new.
This morning, as I watch

the pink cheeks of the baby day
break through the clouds
on the prostrate hills,

she doesn't look like fate,
like original sin,
and I can't help but think

we really can start over,
between fires.

AMONG THE CREATURES

I have a soft spot for the suffering
and make small distinction

among the creatures.
I shoo house spiders outside

not wishing them harm and not wanting
their bizarre poisonings and decapitations

to take place over my bed at night.
I feel for my aging cat

who has developed a terrifying howl
as if sensing his inability

to land forever on his feet.
I don't suppose it's possible for him to know

how important his life has been to me
but I'll be happy if he has understood

my bowl is his bowl.
I easily bond with trees

of many shapes and shadows
and I fall when they fall.

I want to yell out over the chainsaws,
How 'bout that beer we never had?

I do make exceptions for
mosquitoes and houseflies,

returning them to the Great Beyond if I must
but I take no pride in it

unlike the old man down the street
who stands guard at his front door

with a flyswatter,
probably a gift from his wife

tired of hearing
how in his youth he could grab

a fly in the air with his bare hand,
the high mark of his manhood.

All life, like love, it seems to me,
comes into being

with the blessing of time
and the grace of circumstance.

It deserves a shot at sleeping in peace
and rising in purpose

if only long enough to let
its very own hair-raising exuberance,

its peculiar howl,
out of the long throat of darkness.

THIS WELLING UP

I am disappointed to learn
a man was arrested in Canada
for serial kissing. In Canada.
Maybe he was just cold.
Maybe he could no longer
get a grip on his loneliness
or contain a bursting heart.

I could be this guy
on a certain late winter's morning,
hell, on a hot summer day,
all the pretty girls
floating by with their harps,
their lips saying
"Maybe you. Maybe now."

When a man leaves behind
the little boy,
he has learned that
to admire is not always to have,
to want not always to need,
but he is never completely happy
with this arrangement.

Nabokov knew this.
So did Jimmy Carter.
But this yearning, this welling up,
can it be merely lust?
Isn't it moonlight through bamboo?
Isn't it melodies heard between breaths?
Isn't it a wild wind?

But before you arrest me,
let me say this to all the offended,
all the transgressed:
We are supposed
to feel this way.
You are supposed
to be irresistible.

THE CHURCH OF APRIL MORNING

I throw open the
stained glass windows
of the church of April morning,
with its two lonely commandments
of forgive and forget,
its covenant of the hourglass,
its gods of laughter.

April remembers nothing
of the kicked dog of February,
the stubborn mule of March.
In its courageous abundance,
its eccentric grace,
it bursts on the scene
as if from nowhere,
as if death and dying were
distant relatives who missed the boat,
forever lost in short miserable lives
in the old world,
given neither second chance
nor proper burial.

But in our ecstasy,
let us not be seduced by
the dogma of false beginnings,
the charisma of ignorance.
When a shadow April arrives
for the service not yet planned,
remember to pray for
the patience of bulbs,
the fearlessness of pheromones.

If this month be
the cruelest of the twelve,
it's artfully disguised
in the circumambience
of a well-told joke,
for it's mornings like these
we realize why
the Greeks once thought
our arteries were filled with air.

BROKEN

This morning my back is a hungry dog pulling at my pants.
I douse it with pain pills and ice packs but it refuses to give up its grip.

I try a hot and cold shower, deep breathing and stretching on the floor.
I get nothing but a low growl.

I go for a shuffle around the block and only envy the able world.
An old man in lime green Lycra sails by like a flying fish on a bicycle.

A lost soul like a hermit crab on the sidewalk effortlessly shuffles forward his life.
A pigeon with a broken wing hops cheerfully along the gutter, picking up seeds.

So, what's this barking pain of mine, these vicious knots?
On paper, I appear to be healthy.

The doctor just gave me high marks for low numbers,
and the nurses long looks for young desires.

Yet, here I am, a wheelless bike, a tideless sea. I can see myself being mugged
by a six year old. "Would you mind reaching around for my wallet, son?"

As I limp back home, I hold onto the idea that everything has a reason
and therefore everything is perfect, like fond memories.

I pick a fruit from a Mexican lime tree
and press its cool smooth skin against my lips.

The faint musky perfume reminds me of tequila, broken glass
and two girls in a Guadalajara market.

One has a white lily, the other a loaf of bread—
beauty and sustenance, the broad necessities of life.

As a human, I tell myself, I have control over suffering. I can disappear in time
and place. I can wear lime green or go naked.

I am an accretion, a brainy stalactite,
a body full of parts that repair themselves like spring,

which makes me feel sorry for the pigeon with the bad wing.
It cannot hope to fly, not now, not ever.

It is doomed to search for food in the street until it can no longer move,
which does not explain why it seems to love its life so much.

MONDAY MORNING

More deaths occur at 9:00 Monday morning than at any other time.

The Centers for Disease Control and Prevention, Atlanta

I don't want to die
at nine o'clock
Monday morning
backing out
over my dreams.

I don't want to fall asleep
behind the wheel
of the status quo
when I know
I am needed elsewhere.

I want to help the sun
hang its mirrors
in the orange trees
and keep count
for the catalpas
in their tango
with the wind.

I want to be a witness
for the vireo and the lacewing
in their courtship of camellias,
and record the screams of jalapeños
turning green to red
in the clay pots.

At nine o'clock
Monday morning
I want to
fall all over myself
planting a garden
of Tuesdays.

16 CENTS

I went out today
without any money,
not even a dime
except in my
glove compartment
where I found 16 cents.
No gloves,
just a map, a pencil
and 16 cents.

I drove to the park
and walked around for free.
I saw a guy eat a whole
lemon meringue pie by himself.
I watched women doing tai chi
and little kids throwing
sand at each other.
I said to myself,
"It's a free country."

I had no green stuff
because I ran out of it.
Things you can run out of
are different from things
that go on forever.
You can run out of pie
but you can't run out of stars.
You can run out of patience
but you can't run out of hope.

Well, you can say,
"I don't have any more hope,"
but if you look for it
you can always find a little
hanging around somewhere.
A map has hope.
So does a pencil.
And 16 cents?
Hide it in the sand,
and see.

AS LONG AS IT TAKES

The little sculpture of the boy in knickers,
hightop boots and feathered cap
was bought at a garage sale for fifteen dollars.

Someone had removed the patina
so that it looked scrubbed and pale
as if the boy had been indoors all of his life,

as if the boy had never had his boots full of sand
or his pockets bulging with rare discoveries
many of them still alive.

Something had also been removed
from the ground next to the boy,
something he would have cared enough about

to head out to discover with,
a little dog, perhaps,
who would have made him feel less alone,

less scared of this life.
The boy was brought home from the sale
and set in the garden to get his color back,

to give him a place outside
under an old sycamore,
the kind of place a boy might

find a stick and toss it out to his little friend,
the kind of place a boy could wait
for as long as it takes to belong to this world.

TANDEM LIFE

On my wall is a painting
of a young man alone
reading at a table by a tree.
His old rounded house
rests in a wash beneath the hills
like a stone that had broken free.

Hollyhocks pool their pinks
along a crooked wooden fence
near an unhinged gate,
which opens on a path
like a break in the brush
where time and worry wait.

I found this painting
in a corner junk shop where
I came to buy an old tandem bike,
which had a baby seat
and two sets of handlebars
with streamers I had come to like.

I left the shop with both in hand,
one for the tandem life
that wouldn't wait for me,
and one for a rendered life,
a path in painted time,
a place that I could always be.

LONG SHADOWS

Outside the video store
a woman in a *serape*
sits unbathed, unassuming
on the cold cement,
a white cup at her feet
collecting change
like falling stars.

I circle the room inside -
Nickolas Cage the flim flam man,
Kate Hudson the flim flam girl,
Frodo the flim flam hobbit,
but the movie in my mind
is about the woman outside,
the once-upon-a-time farm girl

from Jalisco
or Juárez or Encinada,
whose father and grandfather
raised pigs on field corn
until the soil gave out
and their gums bled
and they fed animals to animals,

and her little brother
who ate the seed with fungicide
and could never go to school,
and the *coyotes* that came sniffing around
promising work up north
but took the Virgin Mary from her,
and poor *Mamá*, poor *Mamá*.

I think about this woman's story,
that movies have been made for less,
that we have ended our own lives for less,
and I walk out the door,
hoping to drop her a wish or two,
but she is gone,
leaving me in long shadows
with a pocketful of stars.

JESUS AT THE CHEVRON

I'm gassing up at the Chevron
when a small man in ragged clothes
shuffles up to me for money,
speaking in a language
I can't understand. Arabic? Farsi?
I think, This is Christmas.
He could be Jesus.
How could I say no!

I pat my pockets for change
but I have none
and hold up a finger for him to wait
until I look in the car.
Not taking any chances,
he lifts up his shirt
to show me a bloody mass
on his abdomen.
It really is Jesus!

What happened? I ask.
Among his next 10 or 15 words
only one is clear to me – tumor.
I pull out my wallet
and rush a dollar into his hand.
He thanks me
and moves on to another car,
this growth that's killing him
now becoming his way of life.

Driving off with a tank full of gas
that probably came from his place of birth,
I wonder what in the world he's doing here
speaking the language of blood and guts,
the lingo of longsuffering,
and I wish I had given him more.

FRAGMENT OF THE DAY

In Miami, a man stood in the trendy market
hungry, unlaundered, transfixed
by the smell of abundance, drinking cup after cup
from a bottomless urn of free coffee
as if he'd finally arrived,
home and heaven having long since
become one and the same.

Outside, an old woman
gathered trash on the street,
trying to force the wind
to make room for her memories
which could include the Latin lover
who never came back
for her opera of murderous proportions.

I stood at the edge of darkness,
thieves stealing roses,
Machiavellian rats in the trees
hollowing out oranges
like Christmas tree bulbs,
dust all the way from the Sahara
infesting my lungs with history.

And slowly, I moved on through,
taking my heart from my pocket
for any who asked,
understanding the other side,
the shadow life,
would always be waiting for
a fragment of the day.

In the car I listened to Chopin,
to his blood,
craving what he knows
about the solitude of truth,
the sorrow of beauty,
and I thought of Elvis the boy,
Picasso the blue.

And Milosz.
How difficult to remain one person, he said.

SOMEWHERE IN THE VALLEY

I decided to get out
of the sick bed,
out of the fetal void,
and see what the world
had saved up for me.

I opened the door
and the first sounds I heard
were the cries of a solitary crow
– "Here! Here!"–
two quick bursts of identity.

Made me wonder why
he needed to tell the world he was alone
on a wire somewhere in the Valley.
Made me wonder
if I wanted to do the same.

I noticed the rain
had fallen all night,
slowly and sleeplessly cleansing
with the brunt truth of gravity
and I didn't even know it.

Made me wonder
what else I didn't know –
how deep the longing among beings,
how broken my marriage
to the rain.

MENAGERIE
At The Little Joy

I arrive at city's edge for a gathering,
the sun collapsing into its own shadow,
the leopard of night circling the crippled day.

I park near an all night market downstairs from padlocked doors
where people exit and drop onto the sidewalk like giant spiders.
A Filipina emerges rocking two ripe pomeloes

like twin golden babies and a lurking grocer nibbles the produce,
curling his caterpillar moustache between suspicions.
A bus pulls up carrying only a cargo of light

too late to revive the day,
now lying in the dust bleeding from its dark wound.
The door folds open dumping a yellow mass at my feet

illuminating my destination.
I slide up the street feeling like a window in a scrap heap,
the fragile dream of escape,

having only a passing experience with the solid
and a still to be determined influence.
Entering a room where the diurnal and nocturnal

are fused into the amber of artistry,
I consider a new identity in this menagerie,
mindful that the spirit of my given name

may dog me for eternity as a poltergeist,
yet liberated by the imagined pleasure of being
unknown but wanted like a scarlet bird.

A MORNING OF NOTHING

I leafed through the paper
and found no news today at all.
The headlines should have read,
"Relax. Nothing Happened."

I paced the floor thinking that
a new idea or an old memory
would rear its radiant head.
Nada. A complete blank.

Something is like nothing in disguise.
It's nothing with clothes on.
It's nothing until
it becomes something.

A pencil is something
that makes nothing something.
An eraser is something
that makes something nothing.

A pencil can make
you remember,
but an eraser
cannot make you forget.

HALF MYSELF

A persistent cawing of birds
jostles me awake on my birthday
like squabbling cuckoo clocks,
and my first thoughts are
that I am late for something.

How I arrived here
with faculties and friends intact
on this path of small failures
and obscure achievements
mystifies me.
So many blind choices
and thoughtless turns
subsumed by the heart,
bereft of conscious heroic intentions.

If entanglements with the
impossible elude me,
perhaps I can suspend
the pending darkness,
starting this day of this year
now fully half awake,
half arrived,
half myself.

As I step outside to get the paper,
a young crow on the lawn
lifts his head assessing the risk factor.
Confident of his pact with the air,
he doesn't need to know
how much I admire his beauty.

ROUSED

Shouts and sirens rouse us from our bed
and we rush outside into swirls of blood-red darkness,
the smell of diesel and burning memories.

It's the garage of the elderly couple down the street
with the ham radio tower and the perpetually motorized son
whose tattooed hands we once hired to rotor a plugged pipe.

Neighbors with folded arms talk about insurance and jasmine
as we return to the house and shut the windows.
I have trouble falling asleep without the sound of crickets.

On these hot summer nights we live at the edge of the sun
careful not to startle the forces around us lest we burst into flames.
So it is I miss you even as you lie beside me.

GUYS WITH GUNS

A guy pulls up next to you
in his pumped up truck
hanging an arm the size
of a rear axel out the window,
a flamed skull stitched
across his biceps for emphasis,
and you think,
"These are the guys with guns."

You want this animal on your side
the day the bad aliens land,
but you don't need to rent
the apartment under him
or let your daughter go out
paintballing with his skinhead son.
You don't make a lot of noise.
You keep your fingers clean.
You buy small and eat green.
So, you know he hates your ass.

It would only make matters worse
if you told him you believed
that vegetables felt pain,
that you were a warrior in a past life,
that you knew for certain there was
a whole class of beings who live
among us in another dimension,
and, no, you weren't referring to him.

Wouldn't you be surprised to learn
he lived the secret life of an intellectual
with a passion for Rimbaud and Kant,
that he collected pre-Raphaelite art,
that he was once married to a French aristocrat
who sang chanson?

Gentle gay poet Rimbaud abandoned
his writing when he was only 20
to become a gunrunner in Africa.
Kant, in a time when Newton was God,
believed the world is mostly what we think it is.

DRY LIGHTNING

In an early morning dream my car
was towed away for overly considerate parking,

dollar bills streaming from my wallet
like scarves in a magic act,

and me breaking down with nothing to blame
but too many years of fire and brimstone.

I woke up disturbed, my day marked,
knowing dreams are pieced together

from anything we cannot make sense of,
cannot own in a waking state,

like being punished for doing good,
which has its own suite in Hotel Hell

for whistle blowers, war protesters
and children forced to go to church,

for Joni Mitchell to spend her last days
as a parking lot attendant,

for Andy Warhol to eat nothing
but tomato soup,

for Gloria Steinem to wake up
in Hugh Hefner's silk sheets.

If being towed is about not belonging,
about occupying the wrong space,

it's not a new thought for me,
having glimpsed my real self once

wandering beside a donkey
in an Aesop fable,

today's version of the story
ending with the moral,

"Be careful where you park your dreams,"
especially your money,

mine coming and going in bursts of
prestidigitation as unearthly as dry lightning,

like the time I gave the drinker
in the downstairs apartment fifty bucks

(instead of the sherry he asked for)
to reopen his long lost shoeshine shop.

Sure, it was a long lost fifty,
but I believed in him and

what if he remembers that,
and the same for the minister of my church,

who absconded with all the funds,
the very man who let his boy

eat nothing but cheese and peanut butter
until the kid's stomach had to be pumped,

leaving me with the feeling that I had wasted
the first half of my life in everyone else's dream,

not understanding that true hell
is having nothing to give.

EXISTENTIAL MARKET

You only come in for a little bread
and milk for your family,

but somehow this question
of how to take them with you

feels like a referendum on values,
an existential moment,

as if the checker were asking
what happens to your inner child

when your identity is stolen,
or what color is life after death,

or who really pays for the NIMBY barge
that left Philadelphia

with seven tons of garbage
and came back 16 years later

from Senegal and Borneo with all of it,
including live Australian pine trees

in the muck that were 10 feet tall.
You know it's not to be taken personally –

she asks everybody the same thing –
it's just the way she puts it

like the Dalai Lama,
as if you'd never thought of it before,

as if you needed to go
in a cave and meditate

only to discover that after three days
or six months or 16 years

on nothing but buffalo milk
and celestial energy

there is no answer,
and you stare at her in silence.

SOUTH OF SUNSET

An old man and two children

were run off the 170 south of Sunset.

He was driving them to school,

their books,

their little white shoes,

now stitched in blood.

How many lives we come to know

through death alone,

their songs heard only by a few,

their purpose bled from our understanding.

With all emotions crowded out by tomorrow,

we press ahead.

Being on the road in L.A. is like

driving around inside a heart

about to be broken.

UNEASY PAIRINGS

Stuck in traffic
behind the firebreathing cars
of basically good people,
and vice versa,
I am cut off,
unsignaled, bad fingered,
completely stopped.

Out my window is a clutter of uneasy pairings —
an empty whiskey bottle
alongside a prayer book in Arabic,
pieces of a tail light
scattered across a little pink blanket,
the remains of a mourning dove draped in a plastic bag
with something unnaturally purple in it.

So it is, how life and death
have it out on the side of the road,
the mr. and mrs. of meaning
squabbling about progress,
about destinations lost
in the great chain
of being and unbeing.

Instead of dying I'd like to be
granted a wish to live on,
killing nothing therefore eating nothing,
therefore throwing nothing out of windows,
a life of good works only —
Jimmy Carter forever young,
Mahatma Gandhi, only better looking.

Here's what I'd do every day:
I'd get up and drink water.
No harm done there.
I'd go out and tend my weed-filled garden
for the poor and the hungry.
And I'd draw little pictures in the air,
letting the wind find a place for me in the sky.

PASSERBY

In the neighborhood of broken glass and broken lives
and empty lots, the old lady in the crumbling house
who feeds the pigeons in the street keeps a garden fit
for kings and passersby like me she'll never meet.

In the neighborhood I hurry through on my drive to work
this spring, calla lilies, jonquils, tulips, mums and bird of
paradise paint the air around this house as if a second
sun could rise.

As seasons change from rain to dust the road too hot
for pigeon feet, these petals, stamens, and showy spathes
never disappoint, never fade, never die, as if the season,
too, were just a passerby.

Then the part of me that knows all things informs
My hurried wishful self, this garden kingdom in the hood
these blooms that look fantastic are made of nothing more
than colored plastic.

In the neighborhood of painted skies and second suns
and different time, the old lady in the crumbling house
who feeds the pigeons in the street keeps a garden
for her dreams and not for fools like me she'll never meet.

LEAVING FOR SOMEWHERE

You live beneath people who fume but never talk,
a rushed and disgruntled gang
of thieves and miscreants up all hours

always leaving for somewhere,
never happy with silence,
never happy with happy.

Last night was one of those
endless arguments with sleep
that made getting up entirely arbitrary,

the stones of yesterday
turning over and over in your mind
until the revelation that

life is the first sign that love is here
casting itself at your feet,
ministering its healing light.

You gather up your brown bag of ideas,
your stained mug of memories
and your stuffed valise of other purpose

and hurry outside toward the car,
your work in the company of others
having become the organizing principle

with its own seasonality,
its own afterlife.
You don't have time to get everything perfect,

so you pray things will be easier
the next place you run into yourself
or else you follow the smell like a shark

in a zigzag toward your target,
which was never meant to be who you are
but what the world wants to say to you.

NO LONGER

The sky,

indecently pale with ghosts

of machines and families,

no longer reserves space

for the toy factory.

Two twisted fan palms

cling to each other

alongside steps going up

but no longer in.

Homeless pigeons

search without clues through

an empty crossword puzzle

of an abandoned parking lot.

A neighboring house,

gardenless and shuddered,

winces in a sudden wind.

FOR US BOTH

You said you never saw
a man eat yogurt

until I dug into a Yoplait at lunch,
and after that you caught me

leaning back in a chair
with a wet tea bag over my eye

and the thought crossed your face,
Should I be around this guy?

Is he wholesome? And I said,
Wait'll you see my doll collection,

then you giggled nervously
and I completed the laugh for us both.

I never got tired of the way
you couldn't hide your surprises,

couldn't stop your neck,
that gossip of desire,

from its early pink display,
or deny your uncertainty,

mirror of a pure heart.
I liked you even as you jogged

through a parallel universe
with air I couldn't breathe,

even as I made plans
for a future you didn't want.

WITNESS

I am not a Buddhist
but to pray over the soul
of a silk worm
for its selfless toil
strikes me as extreme
and absolutely wonderful.

I am not a Christian
but I know that good works
are multiplied
like loaves and fishes,
and I cry
just humming Amazing Grace.

I may not be a Pantheist or a Shintoist,
a Mayan or a Druid
but I'll be the first to bear witness
that the sun is indeed the eye of god
because spring forgives winter,
because prairie dogs have a vocabulary for color,
because your skin guides me through darkness.

AT SOME POINT

As a child I knew the look of death –
my grandfather sliding out of mind
as the lid slowly closed
on his lightless face,
my grandmother strapped
in her wheelchair
talking to ghosts in the window,
a pet duck carried around all day
by the neck.

It wasn't that pretty,
this moon in my blood,
this gravity of forever,
this boogie between bundle of joy
and bag of bones.

Now, viruses sashay through the food chain,
subcrustal crabs serve up my flaking skin,
genes hide behind the curtains
with their pulpy fingers on the trigger.
At some point you're not there
except as memory,
a waltz in the wind,
a photo on the wall.
At some point even the wall's not there.

Anything could have happened.
I could have looked the other way.
I could have lost you.

SCANT LIGHT

Beyond first promises,
the old patterns
never quite stuck with us.
How pathetic we must
have looked trying, though,
you wanting babes in arms
and I chickens in yards –
the lives of our mothers and fathers.

Moving to a cabin in the forest
with nothing but a wood stove,
never having built a proper fire,
frozen to the bone without matches,
the social life of bobcats.

Home births with a midwife
because we didn't know another way,
and taking our little ones
up river in a thrift shop canoe,
then, horrified, stepping through
the paper-thin bottom
as we docked.

Pine trees in the big winds
blowing over like wheat,
and the four of us
planting flowers and tomatoes
in the scant light
of the broken canopy,
as if they'd survive,
as if they ever belonged there.

AT THE LAKE

Your reasons for saying no
were as clear and reasonable
as my hunger to ask,
since no is also the answer
to never asking.

New imaging shows love
to be a craving linked to
gambling and abusing
deep in the primitive brain,
most intense when withdrawn.

Scientists picture
the addicted and jilted
discarding their demons,
pooling their losses,
making amends.

I see you and me
at the lake back when,
throwing our clothes off
and laughing about already
being naked underneath.

GNARLED

She ordered scampi
and I scaloppini,

our alliterative entrées
further uniting

under the same
superfluous marinara

at the old hang out
of Charles Bukowski,

bragged the waiter,
who couldn't have known

I keep a photo
of the gnarled one

on my desk,
his eyes squinting

under a skeptical frown,
a cigarette burning low

in his long thin fingers,
his unimpressed visage

somehow keeping me
from being too self-serving,

too lightweight,
as if without him,

right here on this
merciless street of tony shops

and teenagers with big feet,
I might just go up in smoke.

ROSEBUD

The first person I saw
in the new year was my wife
who lay beside me
coughing and fretting from the flu.

She asked for tea and I included
a rosebud from the garden.

The second person I saw
was a man staring motionless at a wall
as if he'd run out of questions
and found an end to wanderlust.

He didn't look over
and I didn't look back.

A person who gives nothing
will settle for less.
A person who asks for nothing
will disappear.

But a rose will bloom
even in death.

SAYONARA, MY LOVE

Sayonara, my love.
May you return in old shoes,
as they say.

It's your father's gift isn't it,
this wanderlust,
this longing for new air,
new affirmation,
larger humanness?

I can picture him now,
too weak to fight the big war,
wandering Manchuria
tossing out good deeds,
(a coin here,
a tear there),
observing horrors
(soldiers with their
sterile empowerments).

His ancient self must have seen
what it needed of the world,
as if he'd only come back through
for a final review
before the quiet life –
the shop,
the mandolin,
the movies.

He loved old Hollywood,
its wrenching farewells,
its vertical horizons,
just like you,
here on the ground
with your overlabeled luggage,
your starward glances.

Oh, I'll be all right, thanks.
My journey winds internal.
I travel great distances
each time you leave me.

PEARL NEBULA

As if history woke up one morning
and found it had started over,

circling back on its long walk
by the sea before the sea,

surrendering darkness and debris
to scoop up anything of beauty

missed the first time through,
reinventing sensation

like Jackson Pollock's dripped paints,
Bach's equal half steps,

atoms falling into place
the moment they're admired,

frame and form emerging
from light without shadows.

It was here you appeared,
the pearl nebula,

the way Saturn and its rings first
become visible out of nowhere

like the egg of an artic tern
in a nest of dust and ice.

A LITTLE JAZZ

The roar of steamed froth and cellphone gossip
spoil the flavor of my concentration

as I try to write that letter to you again,
the one where I want to ask,

you know, that awful question, Why?
But nothing but spilled milk is left.

Just when I think I could scribble out a sentence
without being scalded,

Odetta comes through the speakers with Amazing Grace
and throws holy water on me,

my sentiments deeply, perhaps irreparably, trivialized.
That woman could hum the theme from Jeopardy and I'd lose it.

You'd think they could put on a little jazz or Bach.
Listen, someday when they have Starbucks

on the new planet Sedna,
I'll finish this letter,

about how we were just out of reach
like a perfect cup of joe.

SEASON AFTER
For Randi

A small book among my treasured tomes
holds a fairy tale from the north country
about a fair lady, a lock of hair, a letter to a young man

with the words goodbye and love forever side by side
just as these two were once upon a time
closer than sky and rain.

Within these covers
lie cloudberries and chanterelles
in the forests of trolls and moose,

grass-covered huts buried
in the snows of Pan and plunder,
red shrimp boiled on the boats

carried in on the narrow fingers of the sea,
and a Christmas tree
made of branches in the wind,

music of old woody instruments
and friends of many worlds, many dreams.
No need for me to open this book

as I stand here on the eve of the holy day
turning the pages over and over again
in my thoughts like a child

who can't sleep until the prince
slays the dragon
and rescues the fairest in the land,

or to read the part
when they stop waiting up for each other
and holding hands in public places

and asking questions that might have long answers
like why he couldn't turn to her
who had always been the first

to keep their hearts from closing at all costs
to reveal small truths
before they rose up like monsters,

or to reach the very end
only to see her disappear in the cold dark air,
their tale forever after entangled in goodbye.

HITTING THE WALL

I loved her like moonlight
even her anger
when I kissed a friend at her party
clumsy and half missing as we danced.

I adored her
as she rushed out the door screaming
dragging my heart through
shadowed streets
to the old cold house on the hill.

I wanted her
as I staggered through the door
and the next door
shouting explanations
hearing my gift hit the wall
breaking into silver Indian beads
everywhere bouncing.

INTO OUR TIME

We were waiting on the platform
between the tracks
for a tram to the university.

I was going over notes
for a test about
Ibsen's *Doll House*.

I lost my balance
and stepped in front
of an oncoming train.

You grabbed my arm
and pulled me back
into our time together.

You still needed me
as flesh and bone
inside your fragile world,

the posts and beams
of your haunted youth,
the crucible you craved

to contain your fire.
I needed the freedom
to be no one,

the freedom,
to honor the darkness,
to be your hallowed ash.

RUNOFF

You've taken a long walk
to the old pond in the hills to listen.
you only hear the fast talk –
an airplane,
a chainsaw,
the arguments of cars.

Then the wind hisses
through the cattails,
two birds bicker in the distance,
a duck fights the water into the air,
and you sit for a while,
arms around your knees.

A pine cone falls through a tree
and you count 1 –2 – 3 – 4 – 5 branches
on its way to the duff.
A squirrel squeals down the trunk to claim its prize.
A bee grumbles past your ear
on its Harley.

You lean back on the grassy bank.
The words that were never even said
roar through the culverts
in your heart like runoff
from torrential rain,
"I can't do this anymore."

THE PROPOSAL
For Kazuko

She returned to school
to become diploma*ed*
in loving essence.
Someday she would be paid
for what she had always given
long before the asking.

Soon, the books she would need
began to arrive like waves of monarchs,
traversing impossible distances,
lighting on our little foldable shelves,
mind by mind,
Muse by Muse,
multiplying into stacks
of unreadable layers,
migrating across the floor,
the stereo, the end tables
and finally, depressingly, the bed.

That's when the broken
fence in the yard
floated its proposal,
arguing that a bookshelf
would be a fine way
for this old pile of wood
to settle down at last.

That's when she noticed
the perfect little space behind
the bedroom door,
forgotten, unadorned
imminently available,
setting into motion
an act of loving essence
between the fence and the space
that quickly migrated across
the floor to the bed
with little more than an arm
for the asking.

ONLY ONCE

We circled each other
among artists in the desert,
in the pale light
along the river of iris and ice.
I appeared to you
in a window in Africa
the year before
you shaved your head for her,
your most brilliant lover.

By then you had
moved to the rain
for the inward journey,
for arms around shoulders.
Still, we found ways
to trade our
teachers and dreamers,
our occasional
backward glances.

Only once did
I question
our agreement
of no secrets
that has kept us literary
and bodiless so long.
Only once did you
mention a scented bath,
that kind of intimacy.

FLIGHT PATH

Like an orchid
you scooped my wings
from the hovering clouds
into your patient capacity.

Gently you embraced
the desperate insistence of my pulse
enfolding my ambitions
in the dust of stars.

Ignorant of my purpose
and dumbfounded by your touch
I knew only that I needed to be with you
in my flight path on the earth.

Through a ballet of petals opening
you released me to dance aloft
somewhere between the heart
and a sky that never ends.

GARDEN TO GARDEN

When I said you float
from garden to garden
in this life
like a painted lady,
I wanted to mean the butterfly
not the geisha,
not the entertainer of men,
but the joyous
wanderer and wonderer.

What would you think
about a walk
on the beach tonight
with Venus coming up on Leo,
you with all the
beeswax and flower oils
that keep your skin
like an apricot in starlight,
you with the heart
that hears outside of time?

JUST AFTER

Maybe you should
dust your bookshelves
at long last,
clean off your Bellows
your bards
your borrowed lives,
redistribute your masters
your whims
your firm intentions.

You'd have to work around
the picture of you and her
looking in different directions,
the mysteriously beautiful moment
captured by a friend
just after the big fight,
and the one of the kids
naked on the grass
holding on to time
as if perfectly content
to be only a memory.

Would it be fair to say
these shelves are your life
or only the life
you allow others to see?
And can you bear to touch
the slender blue vase
she didn't want to take,
the wedding gift
lovely still
though chipped
from so many moves
so many careless displays?

UNFORGOTTEN

Like rogue species of a shadow life,
unforgotten agreements circle back
season upon season,
mood upon mood,

defying taxonomies,
hungering for completion.
Yesterday,
and so many days before,

it was the failed test,
the fumbled ball,
the broken jaw;
your old crippled friend

who sent you away
then swallowed all the pills
you'd left by his bed;
the dog that ran

under your tire,
writhing in the rearview mirror
as you drove on in the twilight.
Then, today,

from your crying silence,
came the girl down the street
who once landed on your porch
looking for sugar and milk

and stayed that lonely afternoon,
the same young mother
you passed in the park
the very next year,

the one with the baby,
the one who followed you
without seeing you,
like eyes in a painting.

FIRST LIGHT

I remember only
the image

not the taking of it,
as if I'd been hiding

behind a blind,
too busy being right,

claiming territory,
plotting next moves,

as if only the camera
had been close to her

in this moment
of undeniable perfection,

my future absence
imbedded in the poverty

of my commitment.
It's the one photo

I keep returning to,
her waist trim

as first light,
her long hair accepting

as a bird accepts rain,
a clockmaker tomorrow.

TRANSITION

What do we really know
　about the animals?
Some people say
　they have group souls.
Others that
　they are teachers
　　who came before us
　　　to give us faith in the turning earth.
We know this:
　They made it possible for us
　　to be human.
　We would not have survived
　　the transition from the wild
　　　without them.
Did they liberate
　our souls
　　in the process
　or do we simply
　　wish it to be so?
How nakedly they express
　their emotions
　and how quickly they rebound
　　from them.
How good they are
　at listening
　and how utterly free
　　they live of regret.
Right after the meltdown
　in Chernobyl
　the bees wouldn't leave
　　their hives
　and the cows
　　backed away
　　　from the river.
If the animals
　are not our first teachers
　then the sterile white blossoms
　　of the apple trees
　　　fell for nothing.

RE-CREATION

It's October.
The earth, exhausted lover,
rolls away from the sun,

and the trees wiggle into their
flowery costumes, dressing up
for another fruiting, gathering, digging

carnival of re-creation.
With the heavy air
of the coming darkness,

no longer needed are the
cool green umbrellas
above the summer fields.

It's October.
The last ice cream truck
of the season

meanders the maze
of empty streets,
its mournful jingle

muffled like memory
behind the turning collars
and closing doors

of migrating ambitions.
In the wind of its passing,
fallen leaves are

momentarily reborn into
winged moments
of childhood.

FIRE

You can't have a little jar of wind
or a bowl of lake.
No such thing as a pet cloud
or a private wave,
or a corner in the living room
just for moonlight.

But you can have
your very own furious fire
right next you
as you read and gaze
and sift your thoughts
through cognac.

Having a fire is like
having a caged tiger.
If you don't feed it
it will die.
If it escapes confinement
it can eat you alive.

But it is not your friend or lover
and you know this on a winter day
holding your glass in both hands.
You know this because fire
you can get back
anytime it goes away.

DANGER OF FIRE

Outside my window
a school bus comes to rest
in the leftover sediment of night
like a giant yellow sunfish.

Little spindly-armed sea stars
hop, skip and wiggle their way inside,
and the fat belly of human potential
wobbles off toward new feeding grounds.

A man at the curb
lights a cigarette on his Harley
and with his first real breath of the day
takes stock of competing emotions and demands.

Exhaling a declaration of disgust,
he flicks a glowing ember into the plumbago
and watches it
until the danger of fire passes.

Dawn arrives already tired,
burnt around the edges
as if serving up
a warmed-over yesterday.

The brown fog succumbs to the heat
and spears of daylight take a stab at some agreement
to bring lenity and new hope
to souls waiting in line for light.

FIRE IN ME

Sitting on the front steps
in the early morning,
pixel by pixel
out of the fog
I try to come into focus with the day.

Buds on the peach tree
slowly lift their pink skirts
to bug-eyed admirers in the sky,
luring them down wing by wing
from those endless circles of indecision.

Geese fly over honk by honk
on their way to boring jobs for the county,
their little lunch pails
full of leftover escargot
hiding beneath their feathers with their feet.

The cat takes its
meticulous tongue shower,
vanishing lick by lick
in front of primordial threats
from passing noses in the street.

If I'm not careful,
with my striped shirt and matching socks,
I could become a lizard on a rock
waiting for the sun to light a fire in me,
moment by moment, year by unfinished year.

A GOOD STICK

I like having a good stick around.
It makes you make more of yourself.
A good stick gives you longer arms
and lets you see around corners.
It can be tough enough
to dig your way out of trouble
or kind enough
to squeeze your hand
like a river rock
or an old friend.

A stick is almost alive.
Like a dog, it'll wait outside
for you to take it to work
or go for a walk.
One thing it won't do
is jump up on your lap
on a cold night by the fire.
It doesn't have to.
A good stick will
jump right in the flames for you.

FEAST OF IMPULSE

A day can turn on
one moment of sweetness –

a first peach in May,
a dog barking at wind,

a child scolding a doll
for not washing its hands at tea.

Or a certain glen
with goldback ferns and

Queen Anne's lace,
where aromas of anise

arise in intelligent wakefulness
to tug at your sleeve,

urging you to pay attention to the stirring,
to gaze into an elsewhere that whispers

"I have something to show you,
something to show you."

And so you leave behind the heavy air,
the bad roads,

guess your way down slippery slopes
and grab hold of the sky

trusting only your call to be there
for the feast of impulse,

the enormity
of life changing its mind.

THE TURTLES OF LA ESCOBILLA

With machetes, the men hack
at the green sea turtles.
They shoot them with long rifles.
They take them away on their horses
whole and squirming in the moonlight.
They dig their eggs out of the sand.
They laugh and drink tequila.

Still, the turtles come back,
ciphers of the earth,
tsunamis of creation,
for 200 million years
a pattern in the void,
raw wet shoulders rising
from the broken shells.

Rising as each man stumbles
in the house to hang up his belt,
rising like the fires of flesh,
crates of carapace,
rising bright and willing because,
like the moon, for most of time
the earth has been theirs.

THE THOUGHT OF BEING

Our cat sleeps all day
on top of a plastic trash can.
The thought of being a better cat
never crosses his mind.
You won't find him
writing down goals,
consulting spirit guides,
hiring a coach.
He's content with
what the world gives him.
If it doesn't come in a can
or have a tail,
it's a total yawner to him.

Anything missing
he leaves
to us big cats
who open the door
when he scratches
the window screen.

PARTY

The beach party
begins the moment
you kick off
your doubts.
The curlews
poke for sand crabs
with their chopstick beaks.
Gulls in new
summer outfits
hunch together,
cranking out tunes.

The sultry sea,
foamy lacy,
misty perfume,
takes one swirl
around you
and your toes sink
into the sandy floor.
Then, dragging away
her skirts,
in slow breaths
and coy whispers,
she asks for the next dance.

TIDEPOOL
For Paul and Sharon

In a tidepool
I found a penny
green and coppery,
its dates gone
as if cleansed of time.

The sea had stuffed it
into a pocket
of shells and stones
where she would take it back
to join her collection of infinite promises.

In the sea
ol' Abe would rise again
through the defiant stripes of parrot fish,
the impervious backs of giant turtles
and the deep cries of whales.

He would continue
his contribution to freedom
through the biology of forever,
wandering the waters
of the long birth.

And someday I will join him
but for now I hold my ground,
too many judgments to temper
and faults to learn to love
in the sea of my uncharted self.

FOOTPRINTS

In the garden
where nature grounds us
with its disregard for our pretentions,
we are weeding.

A startled jay drops its wild berry,
but we continue our work
ignorant of our powerlessness,
intent on ephemeral bliss.

In the rose's petals
lives a family of earwigs.
How nice for them!
So many ants.
So few anteaters.
Love of my life:
What's the plan here you think?

In comes the fog
like a bass note
under the screams of gulls.
We abandon our flowered rituals
to pace by whispering surf,
our footprints fading
like petals of seafoam.

EGRET

Low tide at the holiday finds me

defecting from the gift hunt

to watch life in the tide pools –

nudibranchs, limpets, sculpins,

some of my favorite things.

Suddenly an egret

pops its narrow head

above a mound of sea grass

and flashes a quick

innocent look at me.

I follow it as it wades

from pool to pool

with its big yellow feet

picking over the bargains

like a seasoned shopper.

PANGOLIN

I'm having my usual zoo debate
on the way to see the baby pangolin.
How else would I ever meet up with
such a fairytale African being, I argue?
Aren't we lucky it was found
in a smuggler's pocket at the airport?
But wouldn't the pangolin rather be home
climbing trees with its own kind,
scooping up tonguefuls of red ants and wildness?

I'm certain my ambivalence
is a uniquely human trait,
as I shell out for admission,
concluding that if everything
were left where it was found
I'd still be in Texas –
tarantulas in the frying pan,
dust devils up my dreams.

As I zoom through the zoo
it's easy to picture an opposite world
with humans in cages,
penguin zookeepers wobbling around
sliding fish burgers under the doors,
monkey benefactors with wide gummy smiles
jumping and pointing as we mate.

Finally, I arrive at Little Africa.
The tiny armored anteater is
curled up in the keeper's hand,
a bronze artichoke,
a knight of the night,
tasting its future through a plastic nipple.
We learn that pangolins in the jungle
are sometimes eaten by leopards,
but their true nemesis is man,
who uses their scales to ward off
witchcraft, evil spirits
and other things uniquely human.

How long can the animals hold on, I wonder?
How long can this fairy tale last?

RESTLESS

Outside my bedroom window

an opossum munches on grapes,

his white heart-shaped face

emerging from the vine

like a spirit tasting the world.

You'd think life was unbearably hard

for these foragers,

dogged by gardeners,

dogged by dogs,

fighting their own for their own.

Yet, to me,

the nibbling sounds

in those blushing sweet orbs

calm my soul,

restless in your long absence.

LOLLYPOP

There is a tree in my yard
that loves to grow

more than any living thing,
more than a mushroom,

more than a giant squid.
I cut it back to the smooth shape of a lollypop,

and before I can put away my saw
it looks like Janis Joplin.

It grows so fast during the night that
the motion-activated security lights go off.

By the next morning,
the tree's gone from lolly to Janis

to geyser, circus tent, power plant!
No matter what I do to it,

its big, heart-shaped leaves come back,
reaching out over my deck,

diverting the sun's withering attention
to steal a cloudful of afternoon just for me.

That's why I could never have it bulldozed.
It's the sweetest, most forgiving tree.

It only knows how to grow
and only remembers how to live.

THERE IS A LISTENING

I'll admit I talk to my houseplants
and I'm well aware how desperate that sounds,
but when you talk to things there is a listening.

Today, I asked the queen begonia how she was feeling
after losing one of her most beautiful branches in a fall,
and her answer lay in the paling tips of her leaves,
making me think of my mother's quiet suffering
in the months and years following my sister's final miscarriage.
It had been all I could do not to blame myself.

Cutting the dried flower stalks of the proud anthurium,
I praised his recent procession –
bold red flags above spears of grass!
and noticed that ants from a hole
in the windowsill had invaded his roots.
I broached the subject of a transplant,
echoes of a conversation with my friend
whose failing heart had left him with swollen feet
and the rest of us in the sudden grip of mortality.

The adventurous arrow plant had stacked his leaves
high along the windowpane as if planning an escape into the air,
and I thanked him for his generous oxygenation.
As I turned him around to face the room,
I was reminded of my dad
who used to jump 42 inches straight up,
but arthritis no longer allows him
even to turn and look at me without wincing.

The African violet, a recent arrival,
not from Africa but from work,
appeared to be thriving, and I told her so.
She'd been given up for dead in an office cubicle
and I took her home, knowing exactly how she felt.
Her blue-green mittens were finally reaching for sunshine,
telling me that she was beginning to trust again,
grateful to be listened to, to be heard,
in the way today hears yesterday,
the way morning hears the screams of stars.

DISSEMBLED

In the forest
truth reseeds itself,
as tiny fingers of wind bury
the rotting rituals and decaying conclusions,
and I no longer doubt
that the past can be changed,
privileges remembered,
thought outside of thought.

In the forest
my doubt is dissembled,
unseasonable assumptions
and infertile memories
fail to take root
among the winged arias,
the tendrilled handiwork,
the perennial defiance.

The old cedars sigh
like aging parents
lightening their load with gifts
from their walls, their shelves.
Flowering faces
shout from the path
like street artists
selling their works to the rain.

The voice of my childhood
asks to share this space,
to seek ascendance
for its barbed lineage,
here, where there is room enough
to be still,
to gain strength from the tall ones,
ring outside of ring.

ELM IN DIRT WITH BIRD

Shivering, stubborn, confused,
the hummingbird clung to her nest,

marooned in her tiny lifeboat
of down and spider silk.

In a pruning fury,
I had cut her out of the sky,

leaving branch, nest, and shark-tooth saw
symbolically on the ground

like some kind of protest art:
Elm in Dirt with Bird.

Her eyes followed me
as I comically tied her severed foothold,

home to her sole creation and possession,
back inside the green fountain of foliage.

The ancient surge of April
trembled in her wings,

waiting for Death to lower its head,
waiting for the world to begin again.

WOULDN'T IT BE NICE

In the bowels of brown February
green is a state of mind
as in wouldn't it be nice
to have grass under the big elm tree

when it leafs out on the shelf
of concrete bones and thistles
at the end of the lot?
You could sit outside with your flute

and float melodies in the wind,
birds swooping down
to ride the thermals
of your imagination.

I could take my drawing pad
and fashion a city of pinks and blues
without the stench of the corner grill,
the growl of traffic,

the race against yesterday.
And wouldn't it be nice
if somehow the concrete barriers
of class and race in the world

were removed at the same time
and the noxious weeds
of hunger and greed
replaced at long last

by the gentle green
law of abundance?
Of course, green starts out as brown,
brown being a very different state of mind

as in wouldn't it be nice
if we had a few rolls of sod
on thick clay soil
full of earthworms,

and it was April in the human heart.

CRICKET

A cricket has found its way into my den
and plays its melody thereabout.
I wonder whether it's crying for a friend
or turning my house inside out.

LIZARD

Lizard in the sun:
At my approaching footsteps
Shadow in the brush.

FROM TIME TO TIME

We're rebuilding our rotten deck,
screwing off the top boards

uneasy with what we might find underneath.
No dead animals we're happy to learn,

but a whole ecosystem of slime molds,
ants, spiders, pill bugs, slugs, decaying wood

and little flat segmented guys
must have come from the Paleozoic.

The rest records that blink in geological time –
soda cans, nails, a pencil, a rusty table knife.

Even as the earth shifts and spews
from time to time,

we live our lives on top of others
as others will on us.

BREAK

I took a break from contemplating abode repairs
to lie under the trees on the summer grass,
the cool sweetness of sun through leaves
pouring over me in lemon-lime shadows.

The cat angled its nosebrain in my direction
from its hideout in the ever-waiting weeds,
losing interest the moment it sensed
I came bearing only my own flesh.

An ant tested my will by inspecting my leg
to see whether I was more dangerous or edible
and, if the latter, how many millions of its clones
it would take to spirit me off to the jelly factory.

A mockingbird danced on the roof to complain about
the cat's repeated trespasses, and none paid attention
to the pealing paint on the trim, or the broken cornice,
or the long and deepening crack in the stucco.

As if in collusion with this cabal,
I wondered what would happen if I just melted down.
Hadn't I made contributions?
Hadn't I loved with every chamber of my heart?

These are open questions, closely guarded by time.
With this house, winter has already begun its trespass.
With this man, it's only summer
under a long and deepening sky.

LINGERING STAR

I'm sitting on the porch with a near blank mind
having gotten up a peep ahead of the birds
for no reason I can fathom.

Keeping me company overhead
is one tiny lingering star,
a kid on a field trip to the Chinese zodiac zoo

trying to catch up with his classmates,
having stared too long at the monkey.
It could be me he's been looking at, I suppose,

bored and caged in my own pre-word brain
on the dawn of a big thought but without
the inherent facility at such a songless hour.

I'm a little uncomfortable with this emptiness,
as if it wasn't enough to watch the sky
herd its children along

the path of inextinguishable possibility.
A little ripple of dread tumbles through my gut
like the feeling of not being able

to retract something hurtful said eons ago,
and yet the imagined opportunity keeps returning
in undefended moments like these,

as if time was invented
so I could assign memory to the past
in the hopes of burying regret.

Suddenly, I can almost taste this darkness
now sliced by a thin knife of light
from behind a neighbor's blinds.

OPEN WINDOW

When the sun sets
turning us into shadows,
we crave the ancient order,
a transformation
from nowhere to somewhere,
from me and you to us,
a truth not there until seen,
not seen until named,
not real until held.

Being alive is to organize this chaos.
A Bach fugue does that,
so does a cut diamond, a daisy,
a bird that flies in through the
open window to a world with no sky,
no certain landing,
no familiar enemies,
like in old castle towns
where the streets were built as mazes,
where armies would see the prize
but not the way to get there,
turning back on themselves,
biting their tails like hoop snakes.

Take away our
pacemakers and metronomes
and the world narrates fragments
of fantasies of what we used to be,
like old photographs stored out of sequence,
all emotions conflagrated
into some opera of the past.

We need to trust that
the fire will stay in the oven,
the truck in the lane,
the baby in the crib,
that our songs are whole,
our cells are clean,
and the blood in our wounds
will always return to the heart.

A MOON OR TWO

Has anyone up there
figured it all out?

A place where beings can
bravely assume that all

their needs will be met
so they can concentrate on doing

whatever makes them happy,
on thinking about things,

on taking long walks,
like to a moon or two?

It's supposed to take
nine years to walk to our moon.

1.3 seconds if you're a photon.
It would seem be a steep climb

like Pike's Peak or Machu Picchu,
but it's easy to forget with so

many disappointments on earth
there's no up or down in space.

Apparently, and I'm guessing here,
you would just walk straight ahead,

and whenever things appear to go downhill
you'd lift your head,

the tide rising in your blood,
and continue on the horizontal plane

toward the clean line
between darkness and light,

so easy to define out there,
so troublesome at home.

THE LONG FORGETTING

Let death
be the long forgetting,

the endless disappearance
of singularity.

In these days of light,
I want to remember

all the details of time –
the saucy marching

of the kitchen clock,
heart of the wall;

the baby strawberries,
picked too early

but still sweet as whispers;
the little brown duck

that floats alone on the shelf,
soft, serene,

slowly disremembering
the cries of its wood.

All language came from grief,
said the poet,

the aggrieved trying
to grasp the unthinkable,

the grateful begging them
back to the living:

Let life be
the last word,

and death, if it must,
be our only silence.

ONE ORANGE EYE

News item: The Gemnological Institute of America will for the first time use computers to define what gives a diamond its beauty, the light patterns that create scintillation and the color flashes that make fire.

My computer is a box of
gray matter on the floor
with black nerves
that disappear across my desk
into the wall.

When at rest
it has one orange eye that never closes,
telling me it's only taking a cat nap
and is ready to spring into action
at my every whim.

I even said "I love you" to it once
after a particularly elegant day of
translating the unsaid,
materializing the felt,
formatting the dreamt.

But I never once
asked it to define
beauty, scintillation or fire for me.
We agreed from the beginning
that would be my job.

Today, in a weird and unwelcome artifact,
the rabid eye winked in my direction,
pulling me to the keyboard
where I transcribed
a channeled message.

"Beauty…is…the…mistress of sadness"
came the words,
"the unbearable moment of eternal perfection,
the flower of time."
Not bad for a wire head, I thought.

"Scintillation is
a dreamer among thieves,
a teller of tall tales,
the bastard of radiance."
So, the machine has a mouth, too.

"Fire is beginning and end,
the dance of diamond and coal,
the eye in the mind of darkness."
Ah hah. It's all about itself.
Figures.

I logged off and stood up.
"It's a fine day for a walk,"
I said to the box with no legs,
like in one of those
tasteless hospital jokes.

SELF-CIRCUMFERENCE

I can measure my life in voices along old roads,
music lifted out of fire,
children made to smile in spite of all they know but cannot say.

My accomplishments seem less in number than in hue,
in the manner of a pot of herbs or a comic in the back room
who leaves the few thinking they are many.

My self circumference inscribes a garden of fables,
a feast of nocturnes,
a dream that begins within another dream.

I wear my several selves like borrowed coats
until torn and soiled they cannot be returned
except to the shadows.

I do not know if suffering is fated or random or willful
but there are times I cannot laugh or eat
or make demands for fear of irreversible duplicity.

Just when I am ready to accept
that everything is moving toward chaos,
that love is a demon drunk on itself,

I remember I have seen little girls
dressed up for Easter like hibiscus flowers,
baby giraffes learning to walk on their new stilts,

sparrows building nests in street signs
and I am pointed back to my singular path
where I run ahead madly tossing out seeds,

screaming at death,
keeping time off the calendar in heart leaps,
where even the shadows hide as I pass.

TRANSITORY ENDINGS

I wake up and it's three a.m.,
the ward of car thieves and bats,
my neurons firing like car alarms,
a mesmerizing mandala
of exploding suns in the multiverse –
that approximation of all that is stupefying.

Paralyzed with angst,
I lie here unproductive,
scolding myself for
my ignorance of Eliot,
the new physics,
the old hunger.

I used to look to Freud for answers.
Now suddenly he's passé,
as in "Get over it;
your parents didn't know any better."
Maybe it's time to move beyond
this life of fitful births and small deaths.

Outside it's a cold morning
and I head for the bagel shop.
The heavy door swings open
to lonely appetites and heated imaginations,
people warming up to the future together
like family, like birds.

I overhear maddening fragments of conversation
as in some English teacher's writing assignment.
Finish these sentences and find the story:
"Did you read about that girl with…"
"You wouldn't believe what came out of my…"
"How could we have been so…"

I decide there are only transitory endings,
that whatever happens
is created by everyone.
There is no full knowing.
We are all finishing
each other's stories.

Said Mahatma Gandhi, "If you don't find God in the next person you meet, it is a waste of time looking for him further." People in these pages, some real, some imagined, others misremembered, make possible my journey from I to we, to one. Maybe you know them.

SOME PEOPLE

There are some people

you know you're going to like

even before you meet them,

men who cover their yawns,

women who wear backpacks,

little girls with mud on their faces,

little boys who read,

anyone who picks daisies

or pets stray cats,

the glassman with a purple dinosaur

glued to the tailgate of his truck,

the gardener with an old

"More Trees, Less Bushes" bumper sticker,

the waitress cleaning up

maple syrup all over the highchair

who smiles like it was her fault and says,

"Someday I want to have kids."

EVEN ONE

"It's because the angels take themselves so lightly that they are able to fly."

G.K. Chesterton

There are people who
declare with confidence

they commune with angels
and I do not question their experience

though I have never met such a presence
unless you count the little blind girl

who came by last Halloween
dressed up like a lady bug,

or my unborn child,
or the brother I always wished I had.

I see faces in everything –
wall paper, linoleum, a pile of rags.

I suppose that suggests
I am lonely, and who isn't?

But could it also mean
I am watched over?

If there were angels
why would they be watching me?

Where were they when
the little lady bug lost her eyes,

when my baby was scraped from the womb,
when my brother never came.

If you are an angel
and you are here among us,

lend me your wings,
your rise to higher ground.

GOOD NEWS/ BAD NEWS

A man got a letter that made him sad
The top part good news, the bottom bad.
He read it over and over again
Laughing at the start, crying at the end.
When he couldn't take it anymore
He took his scissors from the drawer.
He read the part that made him laugh
Then simply cut off the other half.

Inspired by a Russian mime.

CALLING BACK

The walking stick
I made my dad
last year is too long now,
time throwing its weight around,
the earth calling back its own.

The tall man
is leaning closer to the child,
to toes stubbed,
holes dug,
treasures found.

Once he transplanted
an apple tree in the rain
coming across
a perfect skeleton
of a sparrow
and clomped
right in the house
with mud on his shoes
to put it in my hand.

If we can chose our heaven
I want mine in the dirt
not the sky,
the dirt of my father
and mother,
the dirt of fallen birds,
fallen tears.

TOUCH AND GO

My dad never caught a fish
and I know this bothered him

because he never said a bad word
except when fishing.

The last time we went out to the lake
you could see all the fat

chrome-plated trout circling
like '57 Chevys at the A&W

around and around our crawdad bait
taking maddening nibbles

but never real bites something like
the touch and go relationship

the two of us had
intensified by the stinky egg sandwiches

he made for the trip.
You could see frustration bringing out

the old captain in the air force
as he threatened to dive in

and snare the "dagnab things"
in his big horsy teeth until

I threw in a wad of eggy bread
and a nineteen incher attacked my line

like a shark on blood
and there was this weird moment

when you could tell he didn't know
if he should be proud of his son

or peeved at the fish
and he just said "shit."

LIMB

On an early morning run
in November rain,

on the ground
beneath a sky

full of beech tree,
my path is blocked

by a fallen limb
big as a lifetime.

I look up at the trunk
and see the scar,

a long, ragged eye
oozing its viscous tears.

I put one of my own limbs
up next to the leafy one and flex,

like I used to do with my dad
to compare my muscles with his.

This fallen limb,
this once sheltering appendage,

is impossibly huge
just like the great man's arms

before his long, slow decline,
his life running on into forever,

becoming inseparable from mine,
from the rain.

SKY

My mother, always little
like a broken toe is little,
like a forgotten birthday,
now is tiny like a tear,
like a fairy.

The only things
keeping her from stardust
are stubbornness
and swollen feet,
reminders of bobby socks,
Missouri summers
and mortality.

She wanted a tall man
she had told my father,
tall as the Air Force,
tall enough to reach things,
tall as truth, dignity
and family.

For her Rhode Island Red
I killed with my BB gun,
for her Chevy I blew up
on the Interstate,
for a thousand Sunday dinners
and sundry goodbyes
and the rude assumptions
of her sacrifice,
I long to leave her with a hug
as tall as the sky
she cleared for me.

My arms feel rough and heavy
as I gather in her shoulders,
so fragile,
like a memory is fragile,
like a paper wing.

EDGE OF TIME

I'm looking out the window
for my mom,
in the rain,
in the brief glances of birds,
in the corn flowers
at the edge of roads
and roads
at the edge of time.

I'm looking out
and over and off
beyond mountains
where memory
gathers in her children
with wide arms of
song and salutation,
synthesis of fire and grief.

She had grown up poor,
being little, having less, wanting naught,
learning to skate on one foot
so she could share
her birthday with a sister,
trying to live on one dream
to give her blood,
her ambition, to my father.

For four days
I stood tall and tearless
beside this lost and broken man,
who loved her like
Kentucky childhood,
like a first peach,
his purpose, his passion
drained in her passing.

For four days
I gathered up the fallen leaves of her life,
the tiny red ear muffs
she put on at the slightest chill,
the Christmas tree pin
she wore the whole month of December,

the old-fashioned ring
my son would have someday.

She died after a bath,
after lunch with friends,
clean, smiling, done with this world.
I sobbed all the way to Chicago,
too loud and too full of silence.

OBITUARY

What needs to be said at long last?
What careful excavations,
what tidy syntax
can bear the monstrous
weight of our missing?

"She had a gentle and happy nature,"
says my father.

Her little sister died
crippled and pleading for another life.
She never knew her brother
who left home young and angry,
consumed by longing.

"She played the violin
and sung alto in the choir."

She was born in a small brown town
with a big brown pond
that had a dock for row boats,
shallow dives,
and long careless thoughts in winter.

"I didn't deserve her.
I could have done more.
I made so many mistakes."

Her mother was a reader
who gave her stories and dreams.
Her father worked two jobs
and slept most of Sunday.

"It's like losing an arm."

She went to a college for women
who wanted to teach boys
how to behave
and girls how to think.

"She was beautiful.
The days are too long without her."

DISAPPEARANCES

In the year of my mother's death
I am obsessed with disappearances –
ideas forsaken,
promises not redeemed,
histories unrecorded.

She had saved her money
for her children in accounts
at companies no longer there,
in policies with agents
long outlived.
I am moved by these
attempted immortalities,
approvals of my birth.

Her closets hung with clothes
once worn by others
for occasions never known to her,
a silent stain on a sleeve
from someone else's spill,
a lost button replaced
by a found one lost by another,
a thread snagged
on tooth or claw now buried
and dissolved of meaning.

In the year of my mother's death
I see faces in the matrix
crying out for time and
memories tucked into spaces
like dust waiting to reincarnate,
and my soul sharpens its tools
like a working stiff
bent on making it to the one mind,
the wide river of light
that keeps the world from ending.

OVER A SHOULDER

How often your death yields to ephemera,
to old patterns of endearment,

the gifting impulse,
like stopping outside a hat shop

and seeing you
in that other way of seeing,

no longer my mother
but Ava Gardner, Lauren Bacall

seducing the mirror in the perfect felt fedora
over a shoulder dropped for effect

then putting it back with the words,
"A woman never gets over such silliness,"

and in the computer store
catching myself rehearsing

ways to show you at long last
how easy to move a thought around

(to go back and start again
like a life imagined).

In the last years
your soft white gloves

had hidden your swollen knuckles
from decades of pounding out Dad's books

at the old Smith Corona
until you couldn't go on,

Dad angry at himself
for how much it must have hurt

and now amid waves of bravado like
"I never would let anyone say

one bad thing about your mother,"
he can't pick up after himself

and I had to find six people to take your place
as if a certain space in the world

would always be yours
like the aura of a severed leaf.

A GUY I GREW UP WITH
For Jesse

Last night we had a beer at Nick's Place
and you knew the best brew to order,
the perfect dish to gnash.

We talked about money
and you'd found the right move to make
and tried to cover the check,

you with the silly cap and big shoulders,
the smart gentleness in your eyes,
but I couldn't let you.

For awhile there
you were like a friend who went way back,
a guy I grew up with,

someone I could say anything to,
except about my first marriage
which I'd kept from you

never knowing the right time,
until it slipped out and you were hurt
because I hadn't trusted you to make sense of it,

hadn't given you a piece of the puzzle
you might already have needed.
All I could say was

how small I felt, how myopic.
For a while there
I forgot you were my son.

THE FALL
For Clay

Gravity is your friend
I tell my little boy,
wiping the blood off his lip.
Roll with it like a stone next time.
Use it like an archer or a rainbow.
Mole or mountain climber,
whale or waiter,
we are all weightlifters under the sun.

Yes, gravity breaks things –
bones, bottles, bubbles even.
No, nothing escapes,
not even your thoughts.
You are as heavy as your sadness
as light as your dreams.
There are fat people who dance like bees
and everyone falls as fast as apples.

IN THIS LIFE

There are things that a man is afraid to tell even to himself.

Fyodor Dostoyevsky

As a boy
I was surrounded by
the coiled muteness of men.
They wore their silence

like winter coats,
enduring the quick tongues of women
like turns in the weather,
wary, yet tolerant, obedient.

It was as though the War
and the Great Depression,
the accidents of their heroism,
the burdens of their survival,

had said all there was
of importance in this life.
When I was eight,
my grandfather,

who lived alone in the basement
and tended a garden
of fruit and beans,
swallowed a bone

from my mother's soup.
In the hospital
his throat swelled up
like a melon

and choked him to death.
I hid behind our overstuffed chair
and heard my father cry
for the first time

as he tried to tell us
what he did not want to know.

SHOULDERS

1.

My grandfather had shoulders like the Cross,
it was said,
a meatpacker from Smith Mills, Kentucky
who was once cornered by a bull
as he cut across a field, __
two nose-flaring charges
two desperate hands twisting the horns
and the father of my father
is pinned against the barbed wire,
too young to die
too exhausted to resist
as the beast,
driven by gonadal rage,
hooves the ground one last time,
takes two steps toward him
and falls to its knees,
its pink tongue flopping out
like a distended clam.

2.

My grandfather had shoulders like the Cross.
The coat he wore
on the day he broke
the wide black neck of the Angus bull
he left behind in threads,
then walked to town
and bargained some future beef
for a new one,
passing by a shivering old man in the street
whom he had once paid in oysters
to castrate his bulls
until the drink finally ruined him.
He returned to the field
and tore his old coat from the fence
and, to the man
who had no coat at all,
he gave the new one.

TO MENTION RAIN

Old Aunt Marthena who lived alone
with her unnamed cats
in a crooked house with crooked stairs
that led to bedrooms of quilt and lace
long unheard and unseen,

couldn't get out of her tub
and lay blue and bewildered
until discovered and told
they would have to move her
to where she could be watched.

Stooped with a hundred years,
she was the toast of the town and
cleared the streets with a big bad Buick
she drove only on Sundays
to speak at the women's club.

From her yard of rusting tools and sentiments
she had always gathered nuts from the old pecan
and sent them in a box for me
with a letter in her steady hand
that never failed to mention rain.

Old Aunt Marthena, sister of my mother, terror of the road
who had owned five houses on the block
that she sold one by one to pay her way,
died before they came for her
and buried her beside her long lost man.

In the lace, in the eves, in the leaves
there were only the voices of rain.

NO ONE ELSE

He was my best friend.

We shared everything
that no one else liked –
the severed rat tail
with legs still attached,
old owl pellets
with tiny white mouse bones,
a set of perfectly functioning gears
dug out of the sand.

Our treasures had numinous force
because they were no one else's.

We liked the movies, too,
and would lay out our popcorn
and milk duds
on the seat between us,
careful never to touch
even a finger of the other guy.

News of his death made me sick
and I stared all day through the floor.

The sky was too big to look outside.

LETTER FROM ELSEWHERE

Like a feral birthling,
you came from the forest
to belong to my good morning,
to contribute to my plodding and insular work.

A slender creature having evolved
whole and unique above the fog,
you had mastery and knowledge
too internal to comprehend, too unique to resist.

Together we shaped the mutual,
creating things that weren't anywhere,
faces neither of us had seen before,
dry and oblique among traces of rain.

I was made larger by you,
with rings of new bone, layers of softer skin,
uncountable wise connections
of canorous arrangement.

You became a voice synchronous to my own,
a thought that finished inside me,
and so it was I loved you
in that way that remained elsewhere.

So it was I found you that day gulping air
as if someone had been holding you under water
and you had come up for a final gasp,
terrified of another dumping.

I remember mouthing something obvious,
something anyone would have said
and how it startled you,
how it was clear you thought you were alone.

Between breaths you told me he had left you
for someone you...*thought you knew...*
so that ... *there were two leavings...*
and no air...and no air....

When I turned to go,
you grabbed my hand
and held it in your mouth
as you began to sob and shake.

I stayed with you
until you released me from your hold,
leaving deep marks from your teeth
and a chill passing through us both.

After you had moved on
I would catch myself staring at my palm
remembering no pain,
being trusted with more than one life.

ABSOLUTELY

My uncle was so absolutely,
so agreeably absolutely.
His car was always absolutely
and so was his wife's cooking,
and the big tree in his front yard,
which was even more absolutely
when it fell in the tornado of '82,
which was the essence of absolutely.

His absolutelies lived and died
in pure absoluteliness.
They were shamelessly, soberly,
demonically, dyspeptically absolutely.
They were equal opportunity,
politically correct absolutely.
He had a glass eye that he'd pull out
and scare all the kids with.
The eye was absolute
and so was the hole in his head.

IN HIS HONOR

I just returned from a funeral for my favorite uncle,
one of those good guys from the good war
who would die for you and maybe did.

He was taken down by cancer everywhere inside his body,
and in the end, he was left with little more
than a disappearing smile, like the Cheshire Cat.

All the time I knew him,
he'd had the big round belly and solid honesty
of a stone you'd want to put in your front yard surrounded by daffodils.

He left three beautiful daughters and a consider-it-done wife,
whose greatest pain might be
that she won't be able to do anything for him now.

He'd wanted a party because he hated the thought of long faces.
She'd insisted on a service because
someone reminded her she needed to grieve.

They'd agreed to have both,
which seemed to me
how they had worked out their differences in general.

At the church, hallowed be thy name, I didn't see anyone crying,
but a lot of people put on sunglasses
after the first verse of "Amazing Grace."

At the house, they served all his favorite foods –
kielbasa, jambalaya, potato salad with bacon
and double chocolate fudge brownies.

In his honor, in his sacred memory,
out of deepest respect for his sacrifices, for the legacy he left us,
I didn't eat a single bite.

ELEGY AMONG SHADOWS
For Cameron

I.
When Don asked if I had ever suddenly not been able to speak as if the words were no longer there, he must have known that his brain was inflamed, that his throat would be empty. He used to say that if Indians had had chainsaws there wouldn't be any redwoods or ponderosas or old growth cedar, and that fires are born to burn, beetles to ravage, that nature cannot be defended and defends itself by surviving. But we all suspected he was a romantic exploring the paradox of his realist's intentions. The bee ties, the brown clothes, the manicured nails were three separate statements that couldn't obscure his impeccable tastes, his opportunist's streak, his refusal to be corralled, not so different from his wild horse of rusty barbed wire gathered from the same old fences that tamed the West, or his Boreins and Quigleys so nicely framed on the wall yet so alive we wanted to dust ourselves off after getting close to them. So, what are we to think of the wild owl that returned his calls and swooped down to feed from his hand, whose claw snagged his glove infecting his blood, whose wings filled the air with terrifying silence?

II.
Don, where are you? Where is that laugh that danced down the painted rocks like a cricket escaped from reptiles, searching, feeling, calling out, wired for survival? Where is that penetrating thought that sawed the table of average minds in half like a magic act, throwing off the red cloak of sunset, the night emerging to applause, arms in the air festooned with stars? In the desert where water turns to sky, where life moves among shadows, you led us from the wasteland of doubt into the beautiful brief florescence of your vision, where questions were excuses for adventure, where seeking meant not to find but to refine the question, where the bleached bones of old thinking were neither the end nor the beginning of a story but signs that the desert served no master, that the desert could gather in its shadows at the season of its choosing. Don, can't you hear the wild air calling? Why don't you meet me at the petroglyphs near the ice caves? I know of a nighthawk there that you can hold in your hands when it's still in hibernation.

THE READER

After old Jesse lost his eyes mining silver in the Techachapies, books became memories and memories a way of life.

I.

He'd seen *The Complete Works* on display at the Palais Royale Theatre. He wanted to know what all the hoopla was about. He wanted to know how long he'd have to wait till he could get his hands on a personal copy. Six incurious weeks in between strikes doing odd jobs for his dad, and the Francis Branch Library of St. Joe County finally got the book back in, which he promptly purloined then hopped the Norfolk Southern out of South Bend to Chicago, finishing *The Tempest* precisely as the train wound out of the wrinkled hills of his youth, and savoring the last line of Sundry Sonnet XXI as the Burlington Northern wobbled into the stockyards of Denver: "These are the certain signs to know Faithful friend from flattering foe." At the first sign of slowing, he threw out his knapsack and dove from the cattle car into the sage, out of view of the guard house at the long wide turn where the Bull would brandish his twelve-gauge and strip the freeloaders naked, letting his German shepherd chew up their boots just for fun.

II.

Twenty-two and living forever, Jesse Tougau brushed off his brown wool trousers and set out on the five-mile walk to town, through the rattlers and hobos in the wash, around the quarry and the tin smelt, past the whore houses, the saloons and the beanery, "hungry as a suck-egg mule." Donning his only Sunday shirt on a Tuesday afternoon, he strolled into the Public Library in Civic Center Park and dropped the Bard into the bin marked Returns. He eyeballed the tables, searched the shelves and lied to the ladies with lines he had rehearsed to the rails: "She is beautiful; and therefore to be wooed," he quoted from *King Henry VI.* "She is a woman; therefore to be won." And so he turned and headed for the oil fields south of town to ply his trade as a caser, that is, before the Santa Fe Southern pulled in and lured him to Borger, Texas, where he'd heard there were gushers the size of tornados and tornados meaner than a September bull, and just before his personal copy of *War and Peace* had worn a hole clean through his brown wool pocket.

THE MOUNTAIN
For m.b.

Having taken a fall into fatefulness, old buddy,
you landed on this outcropping of consequences
called failure. Odysseus in the dark.

The only wisdom you can muster
sounds like it came from a bathroom wall:
'For a good time, call Lady Luck.'

But your dissed dream, your vision of return
is not just about being blindsided by the adverse Winds.
You get what you pay for: Lady Luck is a whore.

How many times can you start over?
This is not a question asked by the daylily.
This is not the concern of termites or tide pools.

This is that moment in the infinite
when you recall ideas can't be counted,
when you summon the desperation of April.

Read those other messages:
Action is the fundamental truth.
For any time at all, climb the mountain.

The smart money says you've fallen up.

FAR FIELD
Remembering Roethke

I listen to the incessant
mowing of grass
that could be
the whispering of wild oats
and the whistling of wrens.

I breathe in
the pale yellows of busy skies
that once had room
for rapture and
endlessness.

What happened to the wild places
of my youth,
of all youth,
where beauty is unowned,
where fruits have continuance?

I long for the far field,
for rocks that squirm,
water that laughs,
and wind that rounds up
her voices like lost children.

READING LORCA

Si muero,
dejad el balcón abierto
(If I die,
leave the balcony open)

Federico García Lorca

Federico,
tonight the moon
is on the balcony
waiting for you.
All of your children
are asleep in the garden –
the melons,
the pale branches,
the olives
from your saddlebag.

She has heard
the coins sobbing
in your grave
and has come to
gather the sacred water
of your quieted books,
your bloodied words,
to take with her
on her eternal
fandango with the world.

Federico,
the moon has come
for your voice.

THIS MORNING I WAKE UP

This morning I wake up
to find the whimsical fog
spraying my neighborhood
with a seasonal flocking,
laying in feathery edges
around all the *sturm und drang*,
evoking the impermanence,
the uncertainty, of being.

My street which just last night
ended in an old apartment
now fades out before the corner
as if the fog were painting over
the sadness there:
Gretta who lost her mind.
Chuck who shot an intruder.
Raymond whose wife is dying.

A stray dog
passing by my window
turns into a legless shadow
then floats out of view
merging with the sounds of children
whose broken voices could be
the little birds you never see
hidden among the half-rendered leaves.

BIRDHOUSE

I keep thinking of that
poor foreigner in New York
who thought he bought
a plane ticket to Oakland, California
and ended up in Auckland, New Zealand.
And the Japanese soldier who
stayed in hiding on Lubong for 29 years
because nobody told him
his side had surrendered.

And the 91-year-old geezer
who got caught stealing Viagra.
It all makes me wonder
if it was such a good idea
to go with the birdsong option
on your cellphone.
When it rings it sounds like
we live in a birdhouse
and your phone's in the trees.

HOME

By the home for boys
trains pass
full of people.
Oh Mommy!
Oh Daddy!

FRIENDS

This room quivers
with the hearts
of friends.
Not even
the cold tea
is still.

VOYAGER

For the first time, a spacecraft is approaching termination shock, the very edge of our solar system.

JPL bulletin

At the edge of the sun's influence
a probe is reaching a point called termination shock –
a lightless unknown,

a realm of pure fear and pure hope
where the past and forever swirl in randomness
not unlike Africa or a celebrity diet.

Somewhere between Somalia and South Beach
I have lost perspective again
and struggle to find a purchase among old standards:

Is anything more important than a hungry child?
If the answer is always "No,"
then it must come with an asterisk

listing other acceptable responses
*a diseased parent, a poisoned land, an ignorant world.
But I'm sick of asking.

All such questions are hostile.
I cannot proclaim with certainty
that we all want everyone to be well fed, fat free,

and liberated from the tyranny of the sun.
Somewhere between terror and decadence
I cast about for common principles and binding compassions,

coming up short sheeted
by SUVs, mutual funds, lattes and lap dancing.
Despite my apparent insignificance

I declare herewith my right to carry the torch
for more humble aspirations –
morning rain, warm embraces and bird song,

taking comfort in the knowledge that
the most brilliant meteors
are sometimes only the size of grapes.

ART IN THE UNIVERSE

Astronomers at Johns Hopkins University announced that the average light from the universe is turquoise. They were wrong.

National Public Radio, March 8, 2002

The average color
of the universe
is beige
it's now declared
not turquoise
as scientists
first thought
but beige
the exact shade
you'd paint a room
for hanging art.

ANYTHING BUT NOW

I'm already tired of the future.
Cloned tabbies that never will be what they never were.

Artificial intelligence that makes it feel
somehow less to be human.

Time travel, as if we weren't
pulling away from ourselves fast enough.

What's next? Friends that never need to be heard?
Books that you eat? Love that you wear?

Don't get me wrong.
I live to see the sky hang up its robe of stars in the morning

and shamelessly bare its pale breasts across the turning earth,
to hear the trees squabbling with sparrows even as

their leaves start new conversations between wind and light,
to feel your hair taking up a corner of my pillow,

as if never quite abandoning the dream of greater closeness,
to walk through the lines of sagging spider webs across the garden

that trace another night of breathtaking circus acts,
to imagine I am that Zen master

who eats when he is hungry and insists
there will never be anything but now.

What happens to us when the mechanical deletes the intuitive?
When time arrives disconnected?

When death skips a generation?
When hearts are posted and pirated in cyberspace?

When did the virtual trump the real?
Why do we need what we don't need?

And why isn't the given good enough?
It seems to work for the rest of creation

if not right now for our friends the walruses
who once gathered on the ice shelves

and howled at passing ships that came too close.
Their ground is melting,

their food is out of reach under deepening seas.
What is, is not always to be with us

who ceaselessly yearn for elsewhere,
for other hearts and times

though here we are part of infinite space
which is, finally, all there is –

unpredictable clusters of energy
spinning through the void

on a journey to a somewhere that is nothing at all.
But the walruses,

that's a different story.
Why would we ever let them go?

IN THE ABSENCE OF THUMBS

*Humans evolved from single-cell organisms to multicellular ones through the
sponge family*

Isaac Asimov

A guy in Punta Gorda
falls down in front of women

pretending to choke so they'll
comfort him in their arms.

A South Korean soccer player
sets himself on fire

soto come back as a spirit
and help his team.

"Absolutely nothing"
sells on eBay for $1.03.

It's not hard to imagine a future
when we humans have overplayed our hand

and life moves on without us,
the whole fragmented people experiment

sent back to the trees –
shopping and soap operas

and supernatural promises
abandoned like so many leftovers,

time, unbuckled from its human wrist,
set free to explore alternatives

to our exclusive brand of self promotion
and logical hindsight.

Who knows what could happen
when some brilliant bird

waiting in the wings
gets a couple of chance

chromosome breaks or a few
strategically repositioned neurons

and steps up like General Haig
to take charge,

declare dominion over us and all?
What unfathomable works

of beak and claw, tongue and tail,
might emerge in the absence of thumbs?

What mythical creatures
in the stratosphere?

What language of
whistle and wind?

Unless, infinity was just
fooling around to begin with,

doodling at our expense,
and the whole sketchbook

gets tossed into the flames,
plummeting life backward

like a nuclear reaction gone awry,
out of the trees and into the ponds,

asthmatic lung fish
reversing their course

and returning to
warm parent waters,

devolving and dissolving
into one big sponge,

a condominium of kumbaya,
simple, soft, without hands,

and all of us,
scammer and scammed,

friend and foe,
together as one again.

JACK COOPER

Jack has written for television, film and the stage. His poetry was chosen runner-up, *Georgetown Review's* 2006 writing contest, and winner, Palabra Productions 2006 National Poetry Month Contest. His poem, "Dry Lighting," was selected as a "strong finalist" in The MacGuffin's 2007 National Poet Hunt Contest, and "Uneasy Pairings" (under the title "Vice Versa") was nominated by www.poeticdiversity.com in 2006 for "Best of the Net." Cooper's recent work has appeared in many national and regional journals including *The Evansville Review, Georgetown Review, The Meridian Anthology, Poesia, Tundra, Poet Lore, Runes, Audience, The Aurorean,* and *The MacGuffin.* He received a Bachelor's of Science at the University of Redlands, a second Bachelor's in psychology and English literature at the University of Trondheim, Norway, and attended graduate school in alpine botany at the University of Colorado, Boulder. *Across My Silence* is his first full-length book of poems.

ACKNOWLEDGMENTS

To everyone whose love and lives are shared in these pages, I am profoundly thankful. This book exists especially because of my family and Muses, Kazuko, Jesse and Clay, author Steve Chandler, publisher and editor Mike Strozier, and poets Ellaraine Lockie, Rick Lupert, Robert K. Johnson and Marylin Krepf.

• *Albatross*, #17, 2005: "Wouldn't It Be Nice"
• *Audience*, Vol. 4, 2007: "This Welling Up"
• *The Aurorean, Fall 2005:* "Re-Creation"
• Bevities, *No. 28. June 2005 "Lizard," No. 38, April 2006, "Good News/Bad News"*
• *California Quarterly, Spring 2005:* "From Time To Time"
• *The Evansville Review*, Vol. XV 2005: "To Mention Rain," Vol. XV1, "The Proposal"
• *facets-magazine.com*, Vol. III, #4, 2003: "Anything But Now," "Passerby."
• *Georgetown Review*, Spring 2006: "Transitory Endings"
• *Glass Tesseract*, Spring 2005: "Hitting The Wall"
• *Goodrichie*, September 2005, Issue #5: "Water On Fire"
• *Harp-Strings Poetry Journal*, Spring 2005: "Tandem Life," Winter 2005: "The Far Field"
• *Ibbetson Street*, November 2003: "For Us Both," Summer 2005: "Open Window"
• *King Log*, September 2004: "Voyager"
• *The MacGuffin*, Winter 2007: "Dry Lightning"
• *Main Channel Voices*, Vol. 3, No. 1, Winter 2007, "Fire"
• *Meridian Anthology*, Vol. 111, 2004: "As Long As It Takes," Vol. IV, 2005, "Lingering Star," Vol. V, 2007 "Season After"
• *Möbius*, Spring/Summer 2005: "A Little Jazz," "Egret"
• *Nomad's Choir*, Fall 2004: "Footprints"
• *Palabra Productions*, National Poetry Month Contest, 2006: "Tidepool," "First Light"
• *Parnassus*, Vol. 29, No. 2 Autumn 2005: "A Good Stick"
• *Pegasus*, Spring 2005: "This Morning I Wake Up"
• *Pegasus (KY)*, Fall/Winter 2004: "Shoulders"
• *Phi Delta Kappan*, April 1976: 'Home"
• *Poesia*, October 2005: "Restless," January, 2007: "Monday Morning"
• *Poeticdiversity*, May 2006: "Unforgotten," "Vice Versa"

- *Poet Lore,* Fall 2005: "A Moon Or Two"
- *Poetry Depth Quarterly,* Fall 2003; Spring 2005: "Flight Path," "Garden To Garden"
- *Red Owl Magazine,* Summer 2005: "The Mountain"
- *Red Hawk Review,* Fall 2006: "Just After"
- *Runes, A Review of Poetry,* 2006: "The Turtles of La Escobilla"
- *Small Brushes,* Fall/Winter 2006: "Existential Market," "Absolutely," "The Fall"
- *Sweet Annie & Sweet Pea Review,* Vol. 11, No. 3. 2006, "Before Dawn"
- *Tundra,* Vol. 4, 2005: "Roused"
- *White Pelican Review,* Spring 2006: "In This Life;" Fall 2006, "Across My Silence"
- *Zillah,* Vol. 5, No. 3, September 2005: "No Longer," "Art In The Universe."

Printed in the United States
71026LV00006B/343-438